Incredible
DINOSAUR
Activity Book

Written by William Potter

Illustrated by Steph Fizer Coleman

ARCTURUS

ARCTURUS

This edition published in 2023 by Arcturus Publishing Limited
26/27 Bickels Yard, 151–153 Bermondsey Street,
London SE1 3HA

Author: William Potter
Illustrator: Steph Fizer Coleman
Designers: Sally Bond and Lucy Doncaster
Design Manager: Jessica Holliland
Managing Editor: Joe Harris
Additional artworks from Arcturus Image Library

ISBN: 978-1-3988-3312-8
CH011482NT
Supplier 29, Date 0923, PI00004548

Printed in China

Back in Time

If you love dinosaurs, then this is the book for you!

Get ready for a daring dinosaur adventure full of activities for fossil fans.
There are **codes** to crack, **puzzles** to solve, **pictures**
to sketch, and a feast of **fantastic facts**!

What Are Dinosaurs?

Dinosaurs were land reptiles that first appeared more than 230 million years ago. They ruled the Earth for 160 million years.

Among the dinosaurs were the largest creatures ever to walk the Earth. These were the plant-eating giants, such as long-necked **Brachiosaurus** (BRAH-kee-oh-SORE-us).

Some fearsome meat-eaters, such as **Tyrannosaurus rex** (ty-RAN-oh-SORE-us REX), were also huge. However, other dinosaurs were as small as chickens.

Not all prehistoric reptiles were dinosaurs. While dinosaurs roamed the land, flying reptiles called **pterosaurs** (TEH-roh-sores) soared in the sky. Several types of swimming reptiles, including **mosasaurs** (MOH-sah-sores), lived in the sea.

Dino or Not?

It's time to test your dinosaur knowledge! Only four of these creatures are dinosaurs. Can you find and circle them?

Allosaurus
1
(AL-oh-SORE-us)

This ferocious predator had a large head and jaws full of teeth.

Pteranodon
2
(teh-RAH-no-don)

This giant of the skies had leathery wings that stretched 3m (10ft) across.

Euoplocephalus
3
(you-OH-plo-KEF-ah-luss)

This large plant-eater was covered in protective spikes and horns.

Plesiosaurus
4
(PLEH-zee-oh-SORE-us)

This long-necked sea monster used needle-like teeth to catch fish.

Deinonychus
5
(dy-NON-ik-us)

This ostrich-sized meat-eater had large claws on its hands and feet.

Iguanodon
6
(ig-WAH-noh-don)

This plant-eater had a large spike for a thumb.

Crocodile
7

This powerful predator has been around for about 200 million years.

Elasmosaurus
8
(el-LAZZ-moh-SORE-us)

This sea creature had a very long neck.

When Did Dinosaurs Live?

Dinosaurs were descended from prehistoric reptiles called **Archosaurs** (ARK-oh-sores). They lived millions of years before humans during a time known as the Mesozoic, which is split into three periods.

TRIASSIC
(250-200 million years ago)

During this hot and dry period, the first dinosaurs and mammals evolved. There was just one great continent, called Pangaea.

JURASSIC
(200-145 million years ago)

During this "age of the reptiles," large dinosaurs ruled the land, forests spread, and the first birds appeared.

CRETACEOUS
(145-66 million years ago)

During this cooler time, the land broke into smaller continents and flowers bloomed. T. rex was a top predator.

Fiery Planet

Copy the dinosaurs into the empty spaces so you end up with all four in every row, every column, and every group of four squares.

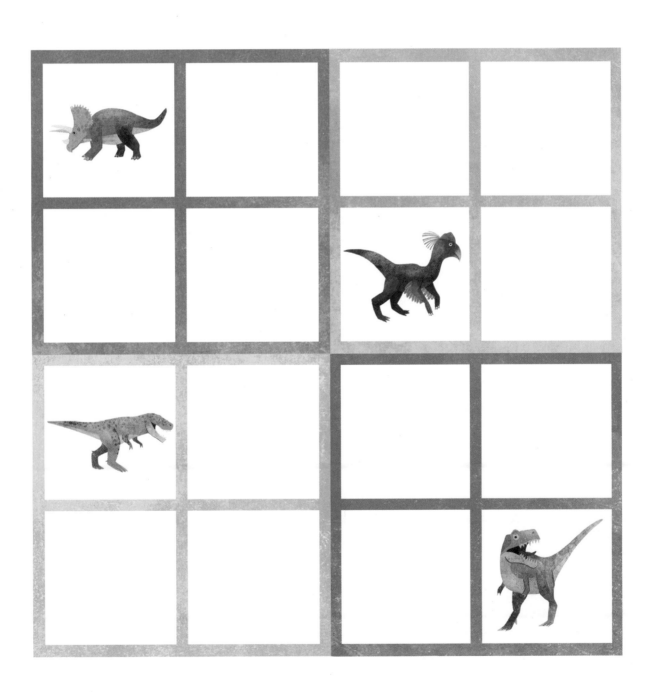

Dawn of the Dinosaurs

In the Triassic period, there was only one large continent called **Pangaea** (PAN-jee-ah). It was one of the hottest times in Earth's history, with mostly desert inland and no ice at the North and South poles. There was no grass or flowers growing. Plant-eating animals had to chew the tough leaves of ferns and evergreen trees.

250 million years ago, all the land on Earth formed one giant continent named Pangaea, meaning "one Earth." Pangaea was surrounded by the Tethys Ocean.

Plants in the Triassic age included fern trees, tough cycads, spiky monkey-puzzle trees, and conifers in the north.

Heterodontosaurus
(HET-er-oh-DONT-oh-SORE-us)

Plateosaurus
(PLAT-ee-oh-SORE-us)

The first dinosaurs in the Triassic period were not giants. Many were just the size of dogs or chickens ... but they could still bite!

Lesothosaurus
(leh-SOO-too-SORE-us)

Dino Differences

Circle **10** differences between these two Triassic scenes.

Triassic Titans

Many Triassic dinosaurs were small—but not all of them! Here are some of the largest, most fearsome monsters living at that time.

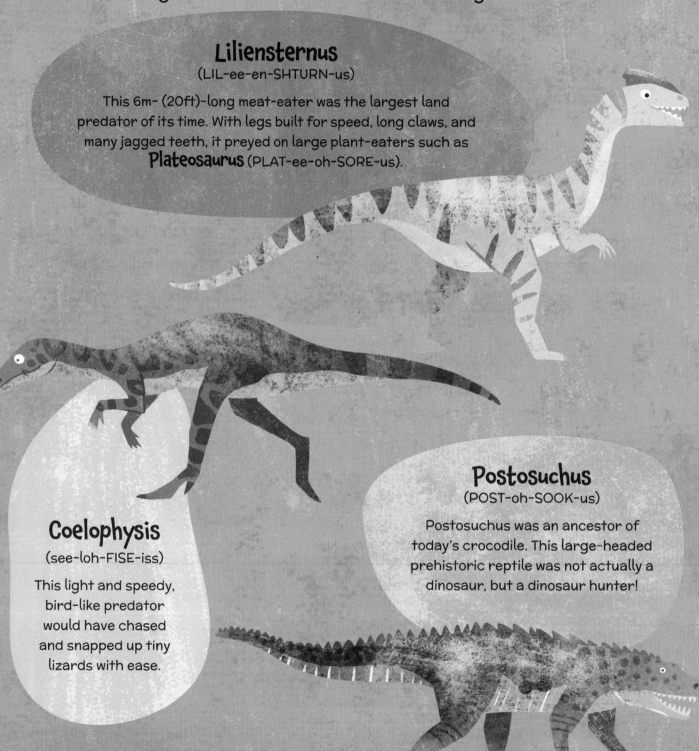

Liliensternus
(LIL-ee-en-SHTURN-us)

This 6m- (20ft)-long meat-eater was the largest land predator of its time. With legs built for speed, long claws, and many jagged teeth, it preyed on large plant-eaters such as **Plateosaurus** (PLAT-ee-oh-SORE-us).

Coelophysis
(see-loh-FISE-iss)

This light and speedy, bird-like predator would have chased and snapped up tiny lizards with ease.

Postosuchus
(POST-oh-SOOK-us)

Postosuchus was an ancestor of today's crocodile. This large-headed prehistoric reptile was not actually a dinosaur, but a dinosaur hunter!

Dino Mosaic

Copy the squares in the right order from the small grid to the large grid. Then finish your picture with crayons.

11   5   9   6

10   3   12   1

2   8   4   7

Plateosaurus
(PLAT-ee-oh-SORE-us)

The fossilized remains of this Triassic plant-eater were discovered in Germany years before the word "dinosaur" was invented. The Plateosaurus had five-fingered hands with a large thumb claw, which it could use for gripping branches, or to defend itself.

1	2	3	4
5	6	7	8
9	10	11	12

Early Hunter

Eoraptor (EE-oh-RAP-tuhr) was one of the earliest dinosaurs. This Triassic creature was only the size of a fox, but it was a fast-moving, fierce predator.

Though its jaws were full of knife-like teeth for eating meat, scientists believe Eoraptor also ate plants.

Eoraptor had long, sharp claws on three fingers of each hand, for gripping and tearing at its prey.

Like many later dinosaurs, Eoraptor could walk and run on its two hind legs.

Raptor Route

Which of the three Eoraptors can reach the lizard through the maze?

Jurassic Planet

During the Jurassic era, the continents began to move apart. Truly enormous dinosaurs appeared and winged reptiles took to the skies. Earth had hot summers and cold winters, and there was plenty of food for both plant-eaters and meat-eaters.

Pterosaurs (TEH-roh-sores), flying reptiles that first appeared at the end of the Triassic, now flocked in large numbers.

Thick forests spread during the Jurassic period, providing food for plant-eating dinosaurs, which grew bigger and bigger.

Along with bigger plant-eating dinosaurs came large meat-eaters, like this **Allosaurus** (AL-oh-SORE-us). This truly was the time of the giants.

Savage Patterns

Many dinosaurs had stripes or spots. Which patterns will you use to bring to life the prehistoric creatures in this Jurassic scene?

Danger Zone

The giant monsters of the Jurassic period had sharp teeth, spikes, and even whip-like tails. To survive, they needed to be very tough, or fast enough to make an escape!

Allosaurus
(AL-oh-SORE-us)

As long as a bus, this mighty meat-eater had sharp claws and a huge mouth full of 10cm- (4in)-long teeth that pointed backward.

Kentrosaurus
(KEN-tro-SORE-us)

Kentrosaurus was a large plant-eater with 60cm- (2ft)-long defensive spines along its back and tail.

Plesiosaurus
(PLEH-zee-oh-SORE-us)

This predator of the sea had a long neck and a small head with needle-like teeth— ideal for trapping fish.

Dino Safari

Can you find all of the dinosaur close-ups in this Jurassic scene?

Jurassic Giants

Diplodocus (dip-LOH-doh-kus) was a sauropod, a long-necked, plant-eating dinosaur, which grew to a length of 25m (82ft). It was the biggest dinosaur of its time.

Able to reach the tops of trees, this giant would grasp branches in its peg-like teeth, then strip away the leaves.

Diplodocus probably raised its tail for balance as it walked. Its tail could also be used like a whip for protection.

Diplodocus had 15 bones in its neck. Each of them was 1m (3ft) long! Humans and giraffes have just seven, much smaller bones.

Draw Dippy

Follow the steps to draw this giant of the Jurassic age.

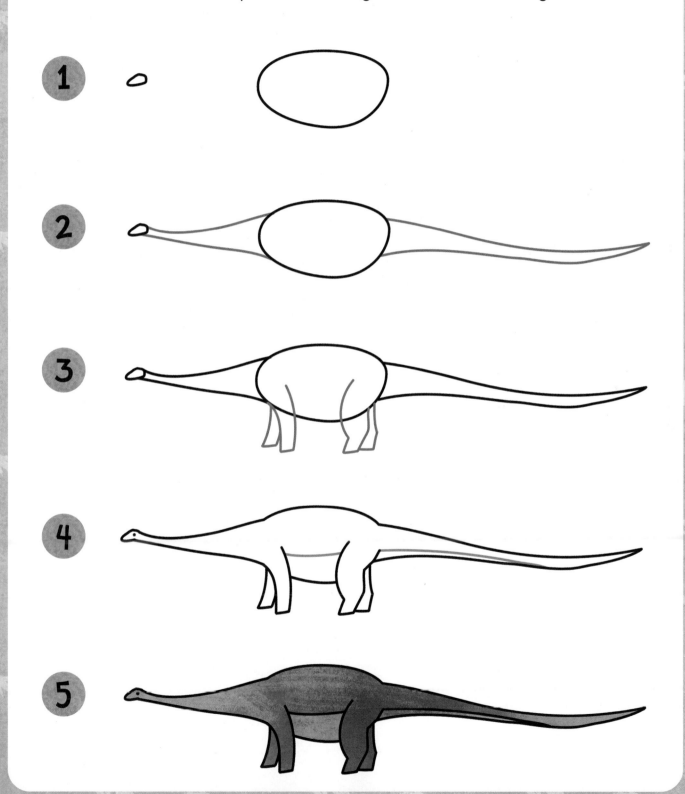

1

2

3

4

5

Rise of the Predators

The Cretaceous period saw top predators such as **Tyrannosaurus rex** (ty-RAN-oh-SORE-us REX) and **Spinosaurus** (SPINE-oh-SORE-us) stalk the land. Gigantic **pterosaurs** (TEH-roh-sores) soared the skies and monsters such as **Mosasaurus** (MOH-sah-SORE-us) patrolled the seas.

During the cooler Cretaceous, the continents moved apart and dinosaurs across the world developed in different ways.

Trees such as oak, maple, and beech appeared, along with the first flowering plants, such as magnolia, for new insects to visit.

The Cretaceous was the time of plant-eaters such as **Triceratops** (try-SEH-ra-tops) and duck-billed dinosaurs such as **Corythosaurus** (KOH-rith-oh-SORE-us). Swooping down from the skies were the largest-ever flying reptiles.

Quetzalcoatlus
(KWETS-ul-koh-AT-lus)

Triceratops

Corythosaurus

Finish the Picture

The top **Corythosaurus** (KOH-rith-oh-SORE-us) is missing his head crest and dorsal (back) spines. Can you draw some on, to match his friend's?

Cretaceous Creatures

During the Cretaceous period, fast-moving hunters such as **T. rex** ruled the land. Even the largest plant-eaters had to be on high alert for danger.

Tyrannosaurus rex
(ty-RAN-oh-SORE-us REX)

Heavier than an elephant, this famous and much-feared predator had a hugely strong bite, with jaws that could crush bone.

Edmontonia
(ed-mon-TOH-nee-ah)

This plant-eating dino was covered in studs and spikes from its neck to the tip of its tail, to protect it.

Iguanodon
(ig-WAH-noh-don)

The jumbo-sized Iguanodon had a beaked mouth for biting plants.

Spiky Spots

Join the dots to reveal a Cretaceous dinosaur
with a large, spiky frill.

Styracosaurus
(sty-RACK-oh-SORE-us)

This massive plant-eater could keep
predators at bay with a large, protective
frill around its neck, surrounded by spikes
up to 60cm (2ft) long. It also had a huge
horn on its nose.

Finned Fright

Spinosaurus (SPINE-oh-SORE-us) was the scariest predator of the Cretaceous period and the largest meat-eating animal that ever lived.

The sail on Spinosaurus' back grew to a height of 1.5m (5ft). It could have been used to attract mates or to control the dino's body temperature.

Bigger than a double-decker bus, Spinosaurus was even larger than **Tyrannosaurus rex** (ty-RAN-oh-SORE-us REX). It had a jaw like a crocodile, with front teeth that were perfect for snatching fish from rivers.

While Spinosaurus caught much of its food in its jaws, the 13cm (5in) claws on each hand could easily grab and rip at its prey.

Scary Shadows

Which silhouette exactly matches the picture of Spinosaurus?

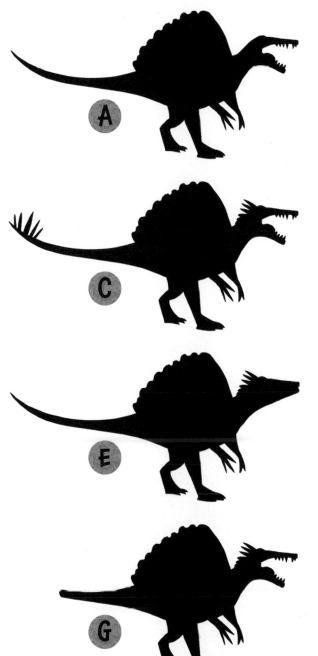

A

B

C

D

E

F

G

H

Meet the Family

Dinosaurs are split into different groups based on their skeletons, shape, and size.

Bird-hipped dinosaurs
Ornithischians (OR-nih-THISS-kee-uhns)

Marginocephalia
(MAR-ji-no-seh-FAY-lee-ah)

This group includes large plant-eaters with horns and frills around the neck.

Thyreophora
(THY-ree-OFF-oh-rah)

These plant-eaters often had defensive spikes and thick, hard skin.

Ornithopoda
(OR-nith-oh-POH-dah)

The dinosaurs in this group were mostly two-legged plant-eaters that chewed leaves.

Triceratops

Stegosaurus

Iguanodon

Lizard-hipped dinosaurs
Saurischia (sore-ISS-kee-ah)

Theropoda
(THEH-roh-poh-dah)

All the meat-eating dinosaurs were two-legged theropods.

Sauropodomorpha
(SORE-oh-pod-oh-MORE-fa)

These were long-necked, plant-eating giants.

Tyrannosaurus

Diplodocus

Odd Iguanodon

All of these **Iguanodons** (ig-WAH-noh-dons) are identical except for one.
Can you spot the odd one out?

A

B

C

D

E

Plant-Eaters

Most dinosaurs were plant-eaters (herbivores).
Here are six of the most well-known.

Triceratops
(try-SEH-ra-tops)

Prehistoric plants were often tough, spiky, and hard to swallow. Triceratops had hundreds of teeth for chewing woody plants.

Iguanodon
(ig-WAH-noh-don)

With a beaky mouth for snipping greens, and chomping teeth in its jaws, Iguanodon could gnaw through most vegetation.

Psittacosaurus
(SIT-ak-oh-SORE-us)

This speedy little dinosaur swallowed small stones (gastroliths), which tumbled around in its stomach, grinding down greens.

Diplodocus
(dip-LOH-doh-kus)

This long-necked giant needed to eat a huge amount every day. It used its peg-like teeth to strip branches of leaves.

Maiasaura
(MY-ah-SORE-ah)

Maiasaura, "good mother lizard," was one of the very few dinosaurs to look after its young after they hatched.

Ankylosaurus
(an-KIH-loh-SORE-us)

Ankylosaurus had a huge gut that got pretty gassy. You wouldn't have wanted to stand behind this dino!

Meat-eating dinosaurs (carnivores) hunted on two legs.
Many had sharp claws and strong jaws for grabbing their prey.

Maiasaura Maze

This Maiasaura mother needs to get home to her babies! Help her return safely by avoiding the predators along the route.

Sensational Sauropods

Sauropods (SORE-oh-pods) were plant-eaters with long necks and tails. Among them were the largest animals ever to walk the Earth.

This huge creature is a **Brachiosaurus** (BRAH-kee-oh-SORE-us). This Jurassic giant had a bony ridge on its skull, giving it an odd bump on its head.

Being such huge animals, the sauropods had to eat a lot of food—about 200kg (440lb) of greens a day! With such a tall body and long neck, the mammoth creatures could reach the tops of trees that other plant-eaters could only stare up at.

Brachiosaurus was three times longer than a bus. Just one of its leg bones would have towered over most adult humans. Its sheer size was enough to keep most predators away.

Forest Feast

Circle **10** differences between these two sauropod scenes.

Meet the Meat-Eaters

Meat-eating dinosaurs (carnivores) hunted on two legs.
Many had sharp claws and strong jaws for grabbing their prey.

Carnotaurus (KAR-no-TORE-us) had horns above its eyes. Its arms were tiny and useless. It had to chase prey and nip at it to slow the target down.

Chicken-sized **Compsognathus** (komp-sog-NAY-thus) would have scavenged on dead animals like a vulture. It could also hunt tiny lizards and baby dinos.

Smart, large-clawed **Deinonychus** (dy-NON-ik-us) would probably have hunted in a pack to bring down large plant-eaters.

Larger than a T. rex, **Giganotosaurus** (jig-an-OH-toe-SORE-us) had 20cm- (8in)-long, saw-like teeth, which it used to tear into its prey.

Irritator (IH-rih-tay-tore) used its long, crocodile-like jaws to snatch fish from streams. However, it may have fed on land animals and pterosaurs, too.

The name of this ostrich-sized feathered dinosaur, **Oviraptor** (OH-vee-RAP-tuhr), means egg-thief. However, it actually cared for its own eggs and probably ate shellfish.

Carnivore Club

Copy the carnivores into the empty spaces so you end up with all four in every row, every column, and every group of four squares.

Terrible Tyrants

The name **tyrannosaurids** (ty-RAN-oh-SORE-ids) means "Tyrant Lizards."
This group included some of the largest, most ferocious predators ever.
They were fast moving, with bone-crushing jaws.

Tyrannosaurus rex (ty-RAN-oh-SORE-us REX) was the largest of the tyrannosaurids.

T. rex hunted, but it also ate dead animals it found. It had a good sense of smell—perfect for sniffing out rotting meat.

T. rex had huge, jagged teeth and powerful jaws. It used them to break through tough skin and muscle, and crunch on bones.

A long, heavy tail helped the large-headed **Tarbosaurus** (TAR-boh-SORE-us) balance as it walked and ran.

These fierce top predators walked and ran on two legs. The **Albertosaurus** (Al-BURT-oh-SORE-us) was lighter than most and could chase faster prey.

The tyrannosaurids often had small arms with two or three strong clawed fingers. They could not even reach their mouths, but they could grip prey.

Tyrannosaurus Sketch

Follow the steps to draw this awesome predator.

Airborne Attack

Flying reptiles called **pterosaurs** (TEH-roh-sores) soared in the skies during prehistoric times. These relatives of the dinosaurs would dive down to catch fish and other prey.

The tiny **Pterodactylus** (TEH-ro-DACK-tih-lus) was the size of a crow. Its short tail and long neck made it a better flier than its large relatives.

As a fish-eater, **Rhamphorhynchus** (RAM-foh-RINK-us) lived near the coast and glided over the sea, ready to snap up a fish in its spiky-toothed jaws.

Dimorphodon (dy-MOR-foh-don) was an early pterosaur with a head almost a third the size of its body. It may have hunted small reptiles.

Quetzalcoatlus (KWETS-ul-koh-AT-lus) was the largest of the pterosaurs. It had a wingspan of up to 11m (36ft), as big as a two-seater plane. Like all pterosaurs, it had light bones that allowed it to stay in the air.

Ptero Tags

Pterosaur names are quite a mouthful. Use the code cracker to decode them.

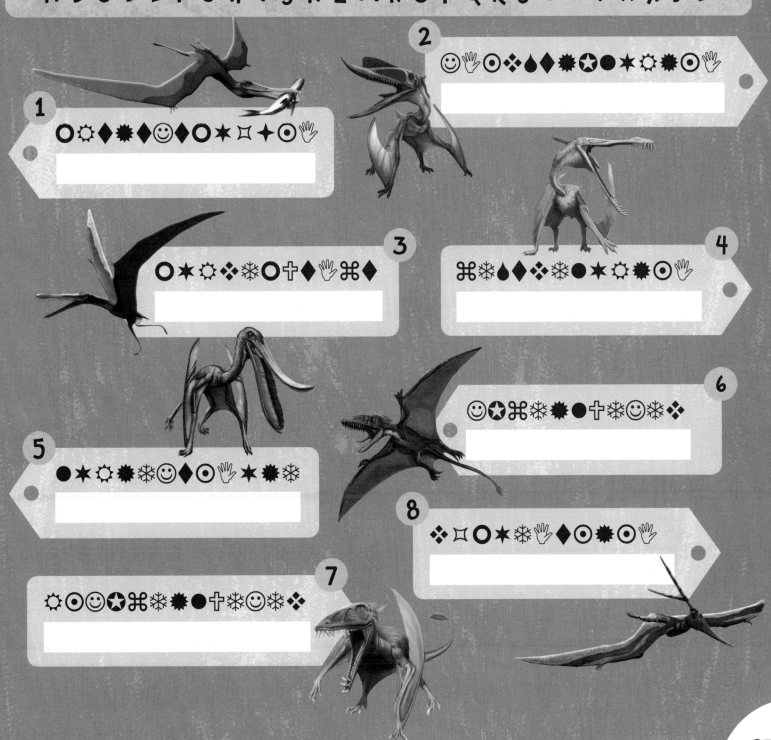

Scare from the Sky

Pteranodon (teh-RAH-no-don) was one of the largest creatures ever to soar in the sky.

Pteranodons flew in flocks. They could flap their long wings but probably glided for longer periods. They could also walk on land, using their clawed hands as feet.

Pterosaur wings were not feathered like birds, but more like a bat's, with leathery skin stretched between an extended finger and a leg. Pteranodon's wingspan was about three times wider than an eagle's.

Males had longer crests than females. The crest was probably used to attract mates.

Pteranodon jaws had no teeth but were like a giant bird beak, adapted for snatching fish from the sea.

Sky Shapes

Which of these nine silhouettes exactly matches the Pteranodon?

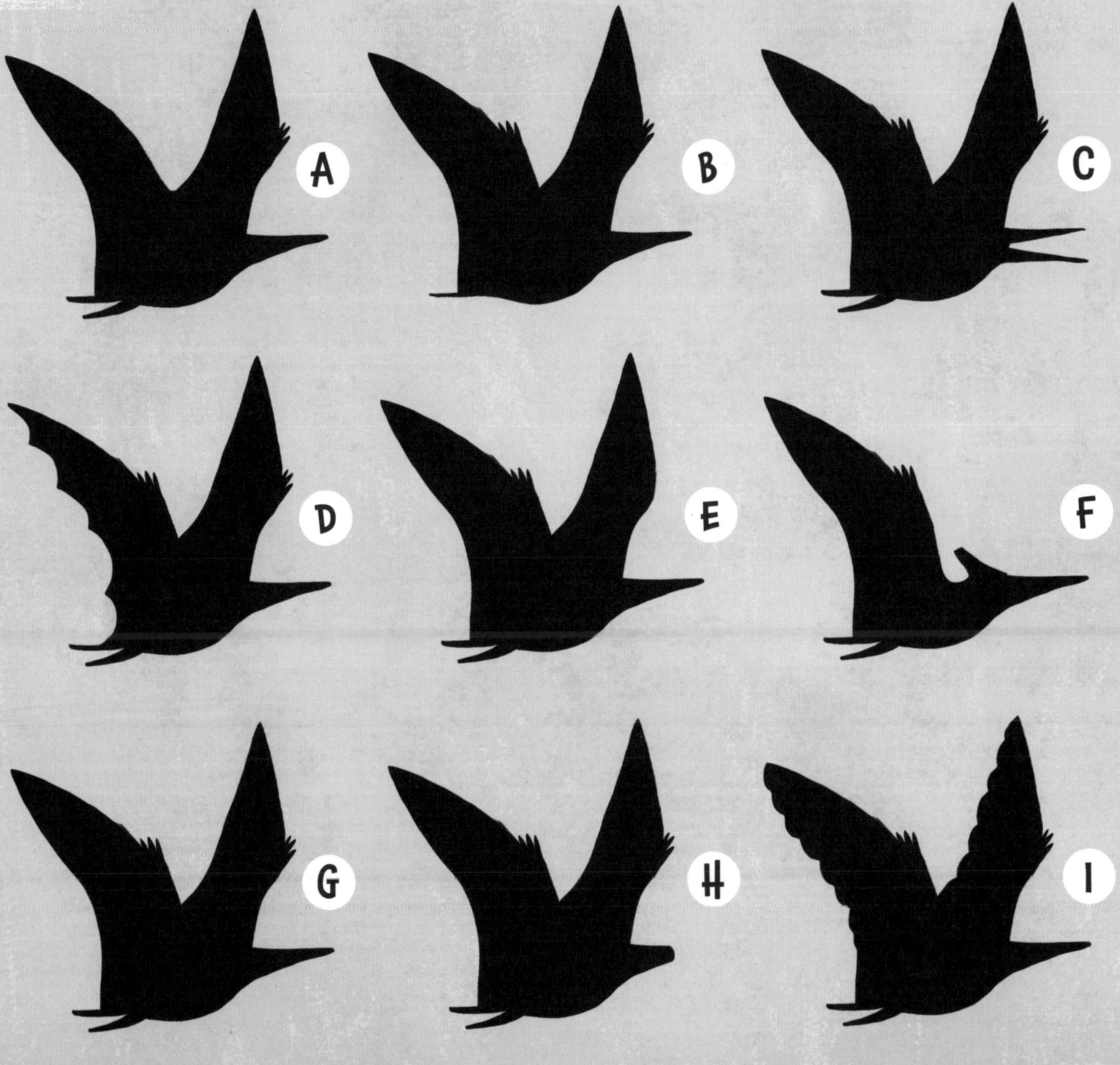

A

B

C

D

E

F

G

H

I

Sea Monsters

The oceans weren't a safe place to escape from meat-eating dinosaurs. Giant marine reptiles hunted in the waters, ready to snap at prey. Here are four terrors of the sea.

Elasmosaurus
(el-LAZZ-moh-SORE-us) was the largest of a group of long-necked fish hunters called **plesiosaurs** (PLEH-zee-oh-SORES). Its neck was as long as its body.

Shonisaurus
(SHON-ee-SORE-us) was one of the largest marine reptiles of all time. Looking like a whale with a dolphin's head, this huge predator grew to 15m (49ft) long.

Whale-like Liopleurodon
(LY-oh-PLOO-ro-don) had a head as long as an adult human's body and teeth as long as bananas.

Hybodus (hy-BODE-us)
was a primitive shark with spikes in front of its two dorsal fins. It lived between 260 and 66 million years ago.

Deep Danger

Can you find close-ups of all the sea creatures shown in the circles?

1

2

3

4

5

6

7

8

9

10

Trilobites and Ammonites

These ancient relatives of crabs and octopuses
are some of the most commonly found fossils.

Cameroceras (KAM-eh-ro-SEH-ras)
was related to modern squid. This giant
creature, at least 6m (20ft) long, hunted
prey with its tentacles.

Trilobites
(TRY-lo-bites) lived
for more than 250
million years before the
dinosaurs. These ancient
relatives of wood lice
were mostly found on
the ocean floor.

Ammonites
(AM-oh-nites) were alive
throughout the age of the
dinosaurs. They lived in a
coiled shell that grew with
their bodies. They squirted
water to move through
the sea.

Escape the Shell

Can you find your way out from the middle of this ancient ammonite shell?

Start

Finish

Sea Snapper

Ichthyosaurus (ICK-thee-oh-SORE-us) was a fast-swimming ocean reptile that looked similar to a dolphin. Just like dolphins, it had to swim to the surface to breathe air. It gave birth to live young.

Ichthyosaurus had dozens of pin-sharp teeth that could snap fish and squid from the water.

Nothing could slip by this predator. Its large eyes gave it sharp underwater vision.

With a muscular body, four paddle-like fins, and a wide tail, this reptile could probably have swam up to 45km/h (28mph) for 30 minutes.

Fierce Swimmer

Join the dots to reveal the **Cretaceous** sea's mightiest hunter.

Mosasaurus (MOH-sah-SORE-us) was the top underwater predator during the late Cretaceous period. Some of these scaly monsters grew to 17m (56ft) long. They would swim slowly near the sea bed, stalking fish and shelled animals.

38
37
39
36
40
1
45
2
41
44
3
35
43
4
42
5
34
6
7
33
8
32
10
9
31
11
12
30
27
26
25
19
18
17
16
28
15
13
29
24
20
23
14
21
22

Mini to Massive

Dinosaurs came in all sizes, from chicken-sized creatures to giants that could step over an elephant.

Argentinosaurus
(AR-juhn-TEE-no-SORE-us)

35m (115ft) long

This gigantic sauropod was four bus lengths from head to tail. A human would only have stood up to its knee height.

Pteranodon
(teh-RAH-no-don)

6m (18ft) wingspan

High-flying pterosaurs (TEH-roh-SORES) lived alongside the dinosaurs. Some were as small as bats, but others were as tall as giraffes.

Spinosaurus (SPINE-oh-SORE-us)

18m (59ft) long

The largest land predator ever had a sail on its back almost as tall as an adult human.

Tyrannosaurus rex
(ty-RAN-oh-SORE-us REX)

12m (39ft) long

The mighty T. rex had a huge bite, with teeth measuring 15cm (6in) long.

Iguanodon
(ig-WAH-noh-don)

10m (33ft) long

This giant plant-eater could have reached the roof of an average house.

Triceratops (try-SEH-ra-tops)
9m (30ft) long

The skull of a Triceratops was one of the largest of all known land animals, a third the length of its body.

Human and elephant

This is an average adult human male, 1.8m (6ft) tall, next to today's largest land animal, the African elephant, which grows up to 4m (13ft) tall.

Velociraptor
(veh-LOSS-ee-rap-tuhr)

1.8m (6ft) long

Despite their impressive appearances in movies, Velociraptors were not much bigger than turkeys.

Stegosaurus
(STEG-oh-SORE-us)

9m (30ft) long

The Stegosaurus was the size of a double-decker bus. However, its brain was no larger than a medium-sized dog's.

Keep Away!

Plant-eating dinosaurs needed to be super-tough
to protect themselves from attacks.

Chasmosaurus (KAZ-moh-SORE-us) had
two long horns on its head, another on its
beak and more around its large frill. The frill
couldn't protect it very well, though. It was just
skin stretched over a bony frame.

Euoplocephalus
(you-OH-plo-KEF-ah-lus)
had tough plates on its back
and a heavy bone club to swing
at the end of its tail, but its
unprotected belly was a soft target.

The **Nodosaurus**
(NOH-doh-SORE-us) had
a back covered in bony
plates. Not being a fast
runner, it had to hope that
its protective plates were
tough enough to put off
any attackers.

Spikes were what kept
Polacanthus (POL-ah-KAN-thus)
safe. These long spines ran all
along its neck, back, and tail.

Code Crunchers

These fossils belong in a museum ... but which dinosaur do they belong to?
Use the code cracker to decode the names of the dinosaurs.

♦ ✌ ⊙ ☺ ☼ ➡ ◌ ✟ ★ ☞ ◎ ✦ ⌘ ❖ ❄ ● ☻ ✹ 🖐 ✫ ◉ ▲ ☹ 🎧 ⛝ ■

A B C D E F G H I J K L M N O P Q R S T U V W X Y Z

1

⌘ ♦ 🖐 🖐 ❄ 🖐 ● ❄ ❖ ☺ ⛝ ✦ ◉ 🖐

2

☺ ★ ● ✦ ❄ ☺ ❄ ◎ ◉ 🖐

3

♦ ❖ ◎ ⛝ ✦ ❄ 🖐 ♦ ◉ ✹ ◉ 🖐

4

❄ ✹ ❖ ✦ ★ ✫ ✟ ❄ ⌘ ★ ⌘ ◉ 🖐

5

🖐 ✫ ⛝ ✹ ♦ ◌ ❄ 🖐 ♦ ◉ ✹ ◉ 🖐

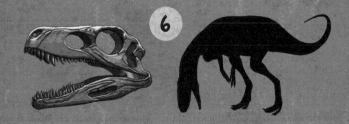

6

☼ ❄ ✹ ♦ ● ✫ ❄ ✹

Tough Triceratops

Bulky **Triceratops** (try-SEH-ra-tops) was a bus-sized plant-eater that lived in the **Cretaceous** period. Its three horns and neck shield protected it from T. rex, which lived at the same time.

The neck frill was probably used for showing off rather than for defending the neck against T. rex bites.

The name Triceratops means "three-horned face." It had two long horns on the forehead and one shorter horn on its beak.

To chew plants, Triceratops has rows of teeth in its jaws. Worn teeth fell out and were replaced. Some Triceratops had 800 teeth!

Build a Beast

Follow the steps to draw this three-horned titan.

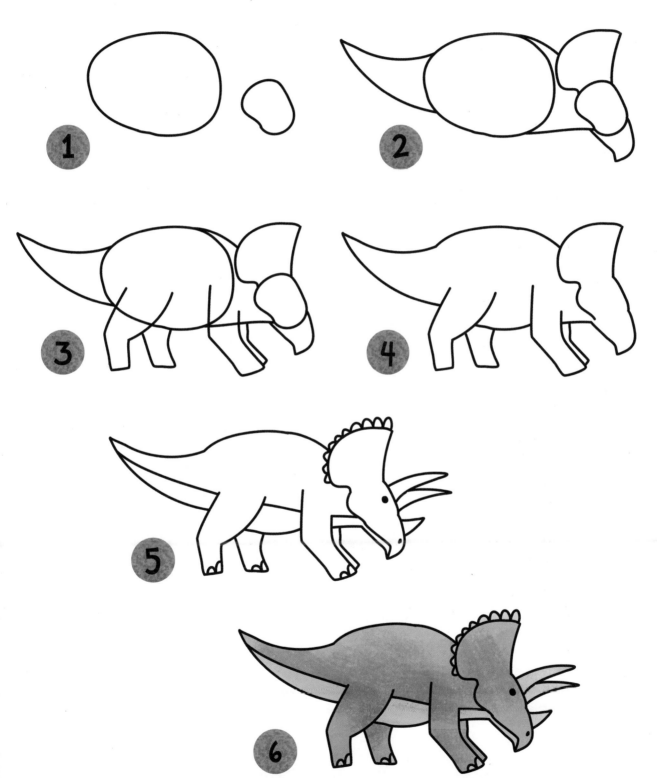

All About Ankylosaurs

The **ankylosaurs** (AN-kih-loh-SORES) were large plant-eaters with protective plates or spikes over their backs and clubs on their tails.

The ankylosaurs had bumpy backs to protect them from attacks by large meat-eating predators. Some were covered in large plates that looked like stones. Others had sharp spikes.

To keep predators at bay, the ankylosaur could swing a heavy, bone-breaking club at the end of its tail.

The head was heavily protected, too. Some ankylosaurs even had bony eyelids!

Take Cover!

Draw spikes, studs, and a club tail to protect this **Ankylosaurus**.

Battle Plates

The **Stegosaurus** (STEG-oh-SORE-us) was a bulky plant-eater with two rows of plates along its back.

The tail had four long spikes at its tip. These could have been used as a defensive weapon.

The diamond-shaped plates along a Stegosaurus' back were not for protection. They were probably used for display or for keeping the dinosaur cool in hot weather.

The Stegosaurus had a very small brain for an animal of its size. While this dinosaur was the size of a small truck, its brain was only the size of a walnut!

Stego-Shadows

Which **Stegosaurus** silhouette exactly matches its fossil?

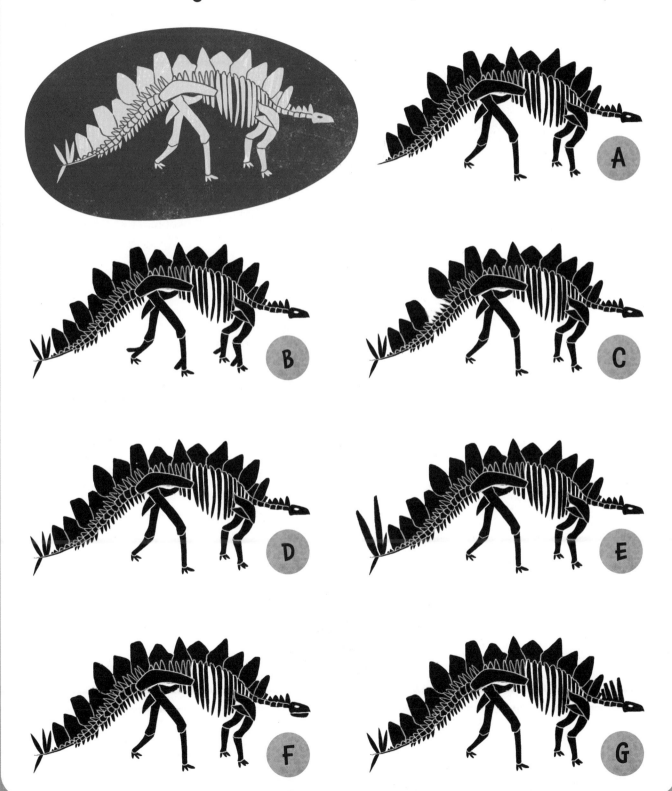

We Have a Winner

Meet the dinosaurs that topped the league for biggest, smallest, fastest, and smartest.

There are several contenders for the title of "biggest dinosaur," but not enough evidence has been found for most of them. **Argentinosaurus** (AR-juhn-TEE-no-SORE-us) is the record holder. This superstar sauropod could grow to a length of 30m (98ft)—longer than a tennis court—and weighed 70 tonnes (77 tons)—heavier than 11 elephants!

One of the tiniest known prehistoric dinosaurs was **Anchiornis** (AN-kee-OR-niss), which was the size of a pigeon, about 34cm (13in) long. It was a bird-like reptile with a long tail, scales, plus feathers on its long arms and head.

Winning the race for fastest dino is **Dromiceiomimus** (dro-MEE-see-oh-MIH-muss), which could have raced up to 60km/h (37mph).

The largest meat-eater on land was **Spinosaurus** (SPINE-oh-SORE-us) at 16m (50ft) long and 12 tonnes (13 tons). It lived millions of years before **Tyrannosaurus** (ty-RAN-oh-SORE-us) and was at least 4m (13ft) longer.

The largest pterosaur was **Quetzalocoatlus** (KWETS-ul-koh-AT-lus). With a wingspan of up to 11m (36ft), it was the size of a small plane.

One of the brainiest dinos was **Troodon** (TROH-oh-don). This predator had a large brain for its body size ... at least, by dinosaur standards!

Dino-Brain

Test your prehistoric brain cells on this challenge from before time. You can find the answers on page 94.

1

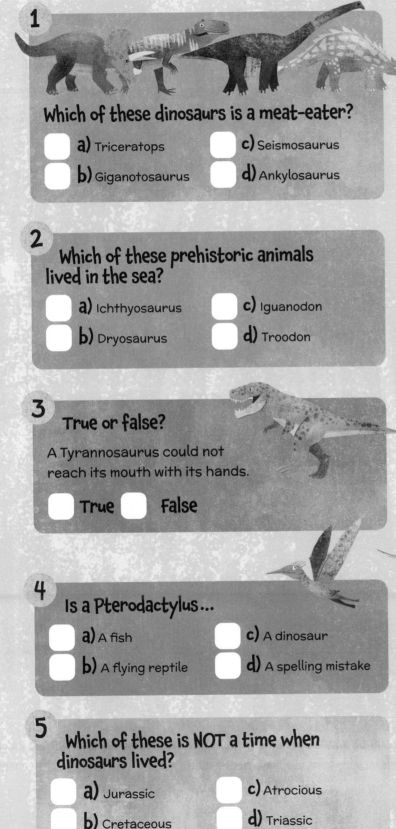

Which of these dinosaurs is a meat-eater?

- **a)** Triceratops
- **b)** Giganotosaurus
- **c)** Seismosaurus
- **d)** Ankylosaurus

2

Which of these prehistoric animals lived in the sea?

- **a)** Ichthyosaurus
- **b)** Dryosaurus
- **c)** Iguanodon
- **d)** Troodon

3

True or false?

A Tyrannosaurus could not reach its mouth with its hands.

- True
- False

4

Is a Pterodactylus...

- **a)** A fish
- **b)** A flying reptile
- **c)** A dinosaur
- **d)** A spelling mistake

5

Which of these is NOT a time when dinosaurs lived?

- **a)** Jurassic
- **b)** Cretaceous
- **c)** Atrocious
- **d)** Triassic

6

True or false?

The huge Stegosaurus had a brain the size of a walnut.

- True
- False

7

Which creature grew the largest?

- **a)** Velociraptor
- **b)** Argentinosaurus
- **c)** Pterodon
- **d)** Triceratops

8

Which of these is NOT a sauropod?

- **a)** Brachiosaurus
- **b)** Diplodocus
- **c)** Seismosaurus
- **d)** Spinosaurus

9

True or false?

Birds are descendants of the dinosaurs.

- True
- False

Crowning Glory

Some dinosaurs stood apart with crests, spikes, and bumps on their heads.

Corythosaurus (KOH-rith-oh-SORE-us) may also have been able to make noises through its crest but it was probably more useful for display.

The curved, hollow crest on the head of **Parasaurolophus** (PA-ra-sore-OL-off-us) may have been used like a bugle to blow a loud signal to other plant-eaters in a herd.

Pachycephalosaurus (pak-ee-SEF-ah-lo-SORE-us) had a rounded skull surrounded by bony spikes. Males may have banged heads together in contests ... and although their skulls were very thick it would still have hurt!

Head Start

Which of these dinosaur heads is only seen twice?

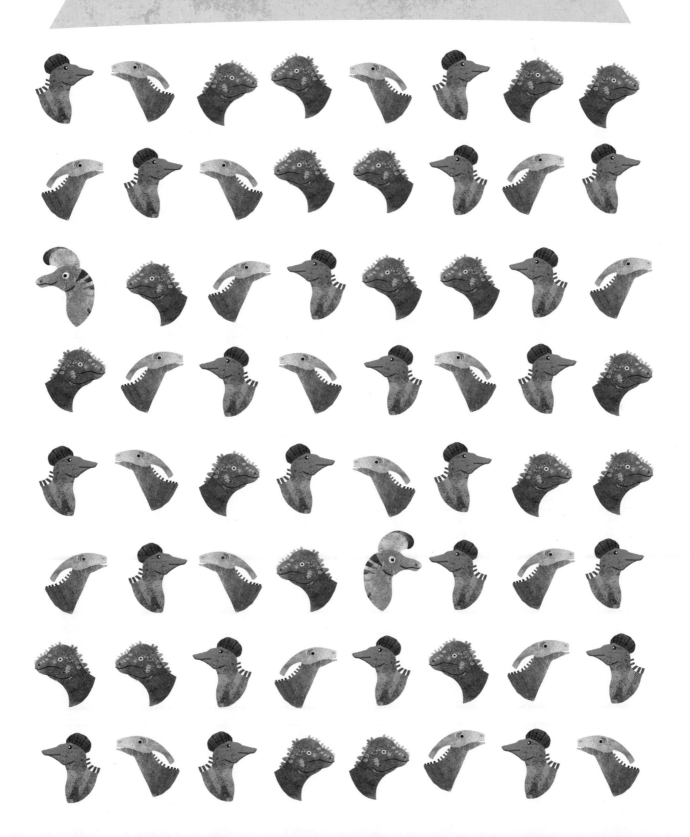

Handsome Hadrosaurs

Hadrosaurs (HAD-ro-sores) had flat bills for snipping leaves from plants.

This is a **Saurolophus** (SORE-oh-LOAF-us), a hadrosaur with a flat beak. The back of its jaws were full of thousands of teeth used for grinding leaves.

Many hadrosaurs, like Saurolophus, had unusual crests on their heads.

Hadrosaurs probably moved around in herds. They were among the last dinosaurs to roam the planet, and died out about 65 million years ago.

The hadrosaurs had small arms compared to their legs, and would have walked on two legs, using their long tails for balance.

On the Plains

Finish this picture of a crowd of Cretaceous creatures.

Safety in Numbers

Living as part of a herd offered protection against predators.

Saltasaurus (SAL-tah-SORE-us) was a large, longed-neck plant-eater. Saltasaurus nesting grounds have been discovered in South America. These huge dinosaurs probably lived in herds and protected their young.

In a herd, there are more animals to keep a lookout for danger, and fight off attacks. Young dinosaurs would have been kept safe, surrounded by adults.

Scientists believe some dinosaurs lived in herds because they have found many fossils together, or footprints of large groups. These dinosaurs may have migrated for food, just as animals such as caribou do today.

Not all dinosaurs roamed in herds for protection. **Velociraptor** (veh-LOSS-ee-rap-tuhr) may have lived together to hunt as part of a group and attack larger prey.

Match Up!

Which of these nine silhouettes exactly matches the picture of the Velociraptor?

Egg-layers

Dinosaurs laid eggs with hard shells, just as birds do today.

Not all dinos protected their nests, but it is thought that **Troodon** (TROH-oh-don) sat on their eggs and kept them warm with their feathered arms.

When young dinosaurs hatched, they would have stayed in the nest and may have been cared for by an adult, just as birds care for their chicks.

Dinosaur nests were usually a bowl dug into the ground. The eggs may have been covered with soil to hide them from egg thieves!

Cracking Up

Draw a dinosaur baby coming out of its egg.

65

Dino Diets

Experts know what dinosaurs ate by looking at their body shapes, their jaws, and sometimes even dino poop!

Meat-eating dinosaurs, such as **Tyrannosaurus rex** (ty-RAN-oh-SORE-us REX) had rows of sharp teeth like small blades, perfect for ripping into flesh. It would have fed on plant-eating dinosaurs, such as **Triceratops** (try-SEH-ra-tops). T. rex had no teeth for grinding food, so had to eat with gulps.

Smaller meat-eaters, like this chicken-sized **Compsognathus** (komp-sog-NAY-thus), would have preyed on tiny lizards or insects. Many carnivores scavenged, eating meat left by larger animals or stealing eggs from nests.

Plant-eaters, such as **Iguanodon** (ig-WAH-noh-don), used the toothless front of their mouths to tear leaves. They ground them up using rows of teeth in their jaws. Many plants were tough and very chewy, like ferns, conifers, and cycads.

Some dinosaurs, such as **Oviraptor** (OH-vee-RAP-tuhr), ate both meat and plants. Oviraptor had a sharp beak but no teeth.

Find the Ferns

Which route should the Iguanodon take from start
to finish to pass the most tasty plants?

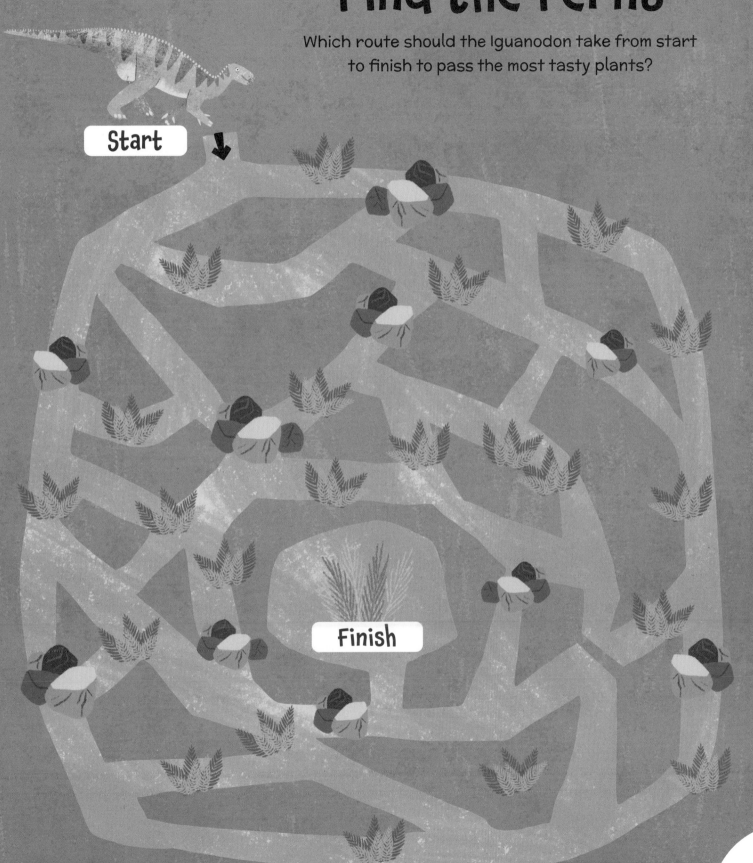

Clawsome

Dinosaur claws were not just useful for fighting other dinos.

The 2m- (6.5ft)-tall **Therizinosaurus** (THEH-rih-ZIN-oh-sore-us) had savage claws on its hands. However, it was a plant-eater, not a predator. Its long claws would have been handy for reaching high branches.

The name of this dinosaur, **Deinonychus** (dy-NON-ik-us) means "terrible claw." It had a long, curved claw on its second toe, which it could use to hook or slice into prey.

The towering **Apatosaurus** (ah-PAT-oh-SORE-us) had a thumb-like claw on its front feet. It did not need claws for fighting, as it was a plant-eater and far too big a meal for most predators. It probably used its claws to hold on to tree trunks.

Baryonyx (BAH-ree-ON-icks) used its 30cm- (1ft)-long, curved claws to hook fish from water, just like a grizzly bear.

Tooth and Claw

Copy the dino teeth and claws into the empty spaces so you end up with all four in every row, every column, and every group of four squares.

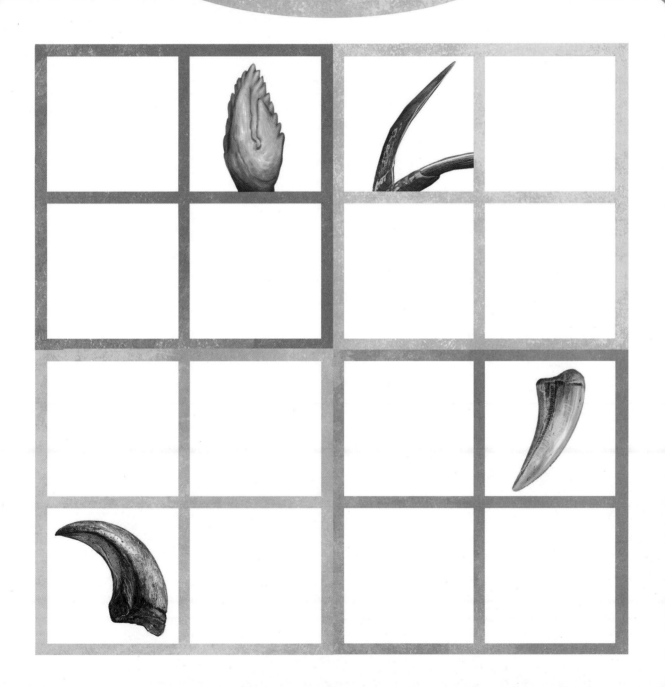

Feathered Fighter

Recent fossil discoveries have proved that some dinosaurs grew feathers.

Though we know that some dinosaurs had bright feathers, we do not know what shade they were. They could have been used for display, just as male birds today show off their patterns to attract mates.

This is a **Sinornithosaurus** (sin-OR-nith-oh-SORE-us), a 2m- (6ft)-long meat-eater that lived in the early Cretaceous. It had a long feathered tail and shorter feathers on the rest of its body.

The feathers on this dino's arms were not joined together to form wings, like those on birds, but they may have allowed the Sinornithosaurus to glide between branches.

Even the fierce **Tyrannosaurus** (Ty-RAN-oh-SORE-us) may have had some short feathers.

Use your best pens or crayons to decorate these pictures of **Caudipteryx** (kaw-DIP-tuh-riks).

The Caudipteryx was a peacock-sized dinosaur. It was a fast runner and had a few teeth at the end of its beak, for biting on both animals and plants.

Dazzling Display

Pack Hunter

Velociraptor (veh-LOSS-ee-rap-tuhr) was a deadly hunter, but it was only the size of a large turkey.

Although it was small, Velociraptor could still cause big trouble by hunting in a pack, as wolves do now.

Recently discovered fossils have proved that Velociraptor was feathered. Its feathers were probably short and helped keep it warm.

The Velociraptor had one large claw on each foot, which it could use to grip and tear its prey. It was also a fast runner.

The top **Microraptor** (MY-kroh-rap-tuhr) is looking bald! Draw some feathers on this dinosaur to match his mate.

Getting Dressed

Early Bird

Archaeopteryx (ARK-ee-OPT-er-ix) was one of the first known birds. It was about the same size as a crow.

The arms had wing feathers, so this small dinosaur could fly or glide.

Archaeopteryx lived around 150 million years ago, in the late Jurassic. This feathered dinosaur flew at the same time as the leathery Pterodactylus (TEH-ro-DACK-tih-lus).

While it looked much like a bird, Archaeopteryx had small teeth in its beak, a bony tail, and long, clawed fingers on each arm.

Taking Flight

Can you find and circle **10** differences between these two prehistoric bird scenes?

Naming Game

What do the dinosaurs' long names mean?

Some dinosaurs were named for where they were discovered. **Albertosaurus** (al-BURT-oh-SORE-us) means "Alberta Lizard," named after Alberta in Canada.

Baryonyx (BAH-ree-ON-icks) means "heavy claw." It's named for the large curved claw on its hand, used for catching fish.

You can imagine the ground moving as the giant **Seismosaurus** (SIZE-moh-SORE-us) stomped past. Its name means "earth-shaking lizard."

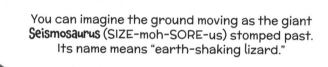

Looking at the **Kentrosaurus** (KEN-tro-SORE-us), you can probably guess its name means "spiked lizard."

Triceratops (Try-SEH-ra-tops) means "three-horned face." Count the horns on its head and you'll know why!

"Raptor" means "thief" and "veloci" means "fast." **Velociraptor** (Veh-LOSS-ee-rap-tuhr) was good at making quick getaways!

Tyrannosaurus (Ty-RAN-oh-SORE-us) means "tyrant lizard." You can imagine it ruling the land at the time.

Who Am I?

Use the code cracker to match the dinosaur names with their meanings.

A B C D E F G H I J K L M N O P Q R S T U V W X Y Z

1
Archaeopteryx
(ARK-ee-OPT-er-ix)
means:

4
Diplodocus
(dip-LOH-doh-kus) means:

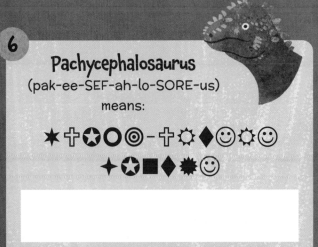

2
Deinonychus
(Dy-NON-ik-us)
means:

5
Eoraptor
(EE-oh-RAP-tuhr)
means:

3
Iguanodon
(ig-WAH-noh-don)
means:

6
Pachycephalosaurus
(pak-ee-SEF-ah-lo-SORE-us)
means:

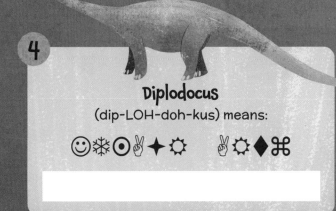

Monsters and Dragons

Dinosaurs have inspired ancient legends and modern myths.

In China, dinosaur bones were once thought to have come from dragons. Fossils of dinosaurs and other animals were called "dragon teeth," and ground into powder to make medicine.

In 1677, an English professor named Robert Plot announced that a huge bone was the remains of a gigantic human. It was later found to be a dinosaur bone, of course!

The curly fossils of the **Ammonite** (AM-oh-nite) were once believed to be snakes that had been turned to stone.

It was once suggested that Scotland's famous Loch Ness Monster was a **Plesiosaurus** (PLEH-zee-oh-SORE-us) that had survived since the time of the dinosaurs.

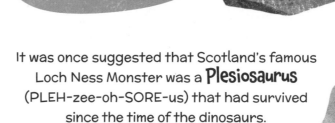

Many films have shown dinosaurs and humans living at the same time, but the giant dinosaurs died out 64 million years before humans walked the Earth!

True or False?

Which of these reports about dinosaurs are true and which are false? The answers are on page 95.

1

Velociraptors (veh-LOSS-ee-rap-tuhrs) only grew to the size of a turkey.

True ☐
False ☐

2

Dinosaurs laid eggs.

True ☐ False ☐

3

Tyrannosaurus (ty-RAN-oh-SORE-us) hunted **Stegosaurus** (STEG-oh-SORE-us).

True ☐
False ☐

4

The largest known land-living meat-eater was the **Spinosaurus** (SPINE-oh-SORE-us).

True ☐
False ☐

5

The **Seismosaurus** (SIZE-moh-SORE-us) used to swallow stones to help it mash up food in its stomach.

True ☐
False ☐

6

The word "dinosaur" translates as "terrible lizard."

True ☐
False ☐

7

The largest known animal to have ever lived was a dinosaur.

True ☐ False ☐

8

The **Diplodocus** (dip-LOH-doh-kus) was a fierce predator that hunted smaller dinosaurs.

True ☐
False ☐

Skeleton Skills

Fossilized skeletons can tell us a lot about how the dinosaurs lived.

This is the fossilized skeleton of a **Tyrannosaurus** (Ty-RAN-oh-SORE-us). The size of its skull, and the number and shape of its teeth show this dino was a meat-eater, built to take big chunks out of other creatures.

This dino has hips like those of a lizard. T. rex is a **theropod** (THEH-roh-pod), a dinosaur that walked on two legs, not four.

The arms are very tiny compared to the legs and could only have been used for gripping, not for feeding.

The tail would have helped balance the Tyrannosaurus when it was running after prey.

Lost Bones

All of these T. rex skeletons are missing one bone. Work out where the missing bones should be by comparing the skeletons.

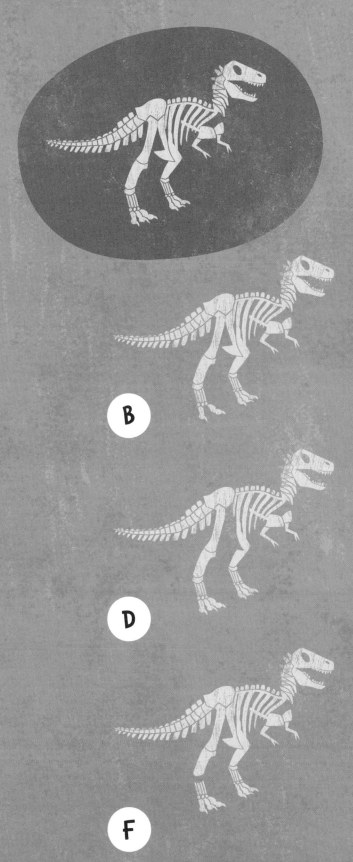

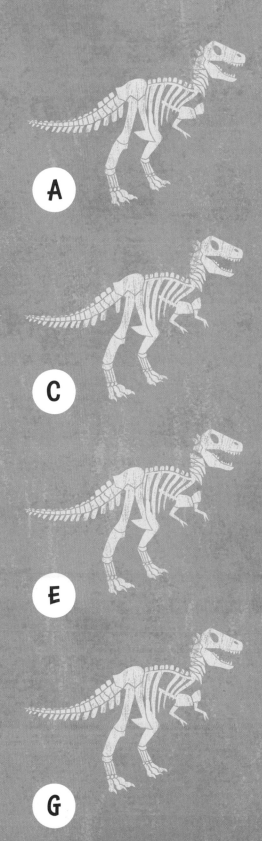

Forming Fossils

Fossils are the remains of dinosaurs that died out millions of years ago.

Many dinosaurs died and were eaten by other dinosaurs, but some were buried under layers of mud.

The soft parts of the body decayed, leaving just the skeleton.

Over millions of years, the bones were turned to stone as chemicals soaked into them.

The rocky skeleton, called a **fossil**, was squashed under many layers of soil and rock, then discovered and dug up by dinosaur experts.

Fake a Fossil

Here's how to make your own fabulous fossil.

What you need:

A small dinosaur toy

Toy clay

Bowl

Plaster of Paris

Water

Acrylic paints

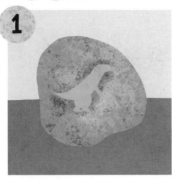

1

Press your dinosaur toy in a large ball of toy clay, to leave a deep imprint.

2

Build a wall of clay around your dino print.

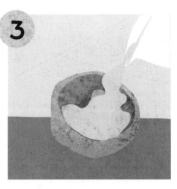

3

Pour the mixed plaster into the clay. Leave it to dry.

4

Remove the clay from the plaster to reveal your fossil. Decorate it with paint.

Digging Dinosaurs

Fossils are hidden under layers of rock, waiting to be discovered.

Some fossils are discovered by accident during digging work. Others are found by experts, called **paleontologists** (PAY-lee-on-TOH-loh-jists), exploring a site known for fossils.

The fossilized bones are carefully dug out from the rock with hammers, drills, and chisels. Brushes are used to wipe away any dust.

Once a fossil is found, measurements and photos are taken to record its position.

The fossils are wrapped in plaster of Paris to protect them on their journey to a laboratory, where they will be studied or put together for a museum display.

Right Remains

Where do these fossil pieces fit on this large dinosaur skeleton?

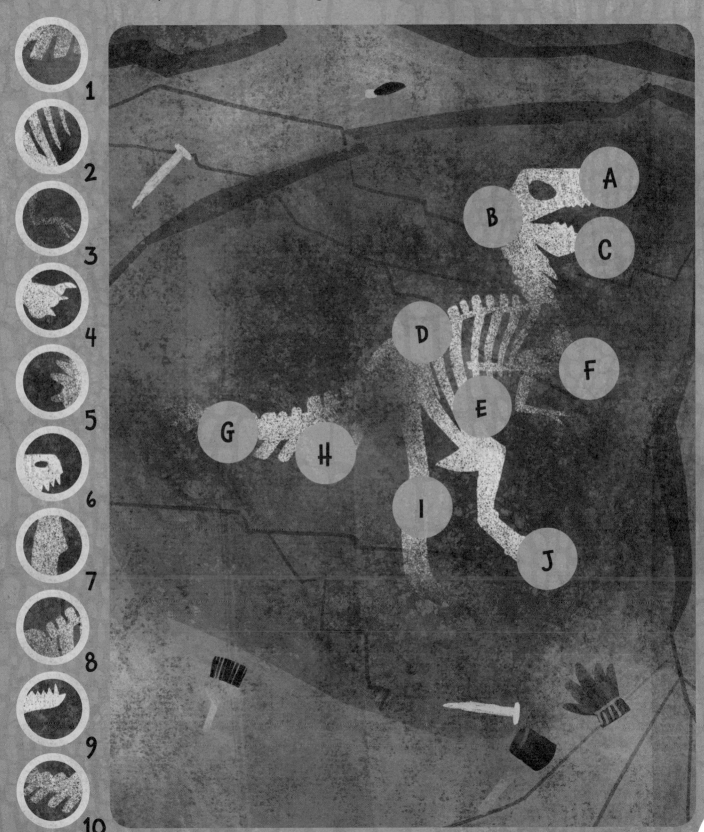

End of the Dinosaurs

The dinosaurs disappeared from the planet about 65 million years ago. But what happened to them?

Scientists believe that a huge meteor, 10km (6.2 miles) wide, hit the Earth on the coast of Mexico 65 million years ago.

This disaster helped cause the end of the dinosaurs and pterosaurs, but some creatures survived, including sharks, crocodiles, mammals, birds, and insects.

The meteor impact would have caused the sky to fill up with dust and smoke, blocking out sunlight.

Without sunlight, plants died and the world grew cold, making it impossible for many creatures to survive.

Fleeing the Fire

Decorate this **pterosaur** (TEH-roh-sore) as it tries to escape from the fiery volcano.

Dinos Today

The descendants of dinosaurs are still alive!

Birds descended from theropod dinosaurs, such as **Velociraptor** (veh-LOSS-ee-rap-tuhr). Over millions of years, they lost their teeth and bony tails to become the birds we know today.

The hoatzin is a pheasant-sized bird from South America that looks a lot like its prehistoric ancestors. As a chick, it has claws on its wings, which it uses to climb trees. That's just like an **Archaeopteryx** (ARK-ee-OPT-er-ix)!

Compare this living cassowary with an **Oviraptor** (OH-vee-RAP-tor). Do you think they look similar?

Crocodiles look very like prehistoric monsters. They are descended from **archosaurs** (ARK-oh-sores), the creatures that came before dinosaurs.

Sharks, turtles, and snakes were around at the time of the dinosaurs and are still alive today.

Chomping Card

Add bite to a birthday with this snappy dinosaur card.

What you need:

Two sheets of card
(one red, one green)

A pair of scissors

Glue

Marker pen

1

Fold both sheets
of card in half.

open end

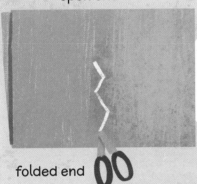

folded end

2

Cut a zigzag line in
the green paper, like
this. Stop when you
reach the middle of
the paper.

3

Make diagonal folds on
both sides of the zigzag,
following the dotted lines
shown here. Crease the
folds both ways.

4

Now open the paper and
push the jaws forward
to make them snap! Then
draw a dinosaur head
around the mouth.

5

Glue the edges
of the green
card inside the
red card to finish
your pop-up
dino card.

Answers

Don't read these pages until you have
tried the puzzles for yourself.
No peeking!

Page 5: Dino or Not?

These are dinosaurs:

1. Allosaurus
3. Euoplocephalus
5. Deinonychus
6. Iguanodon

Page 7: Fiery Planet

Page 9: Dino Differences

Page 11: Dino Mosaic

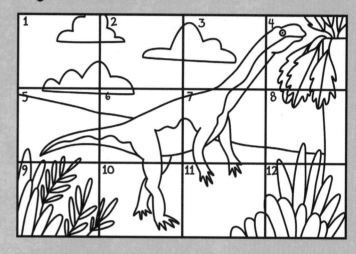

Page 13: Raptor Route

Answer: C

Page 17: Dino Safari

Page 23: Spiky Spots

Page 25: Scary Shadows
Answer: F

Page 27: Odd Iguanodon
Answer: C

Page 29: Maiasaura Maze

Page 31: Forest Feast

Page 33: Carnivore Club

Page 37: Ptero Tags

Decoded dinosaur names:

1. Cearadactytus
2. Dsungaripterus
3. Ctenochasma
4. Moganopterus
5. Pterodaustro
6. Dimorphodon
7. Eudimorphodon
8. Nyctosaurus

Page 39: Sky Shapes

Answer: G

Page 43: Escape the Shell

Page 41: Deep Danger

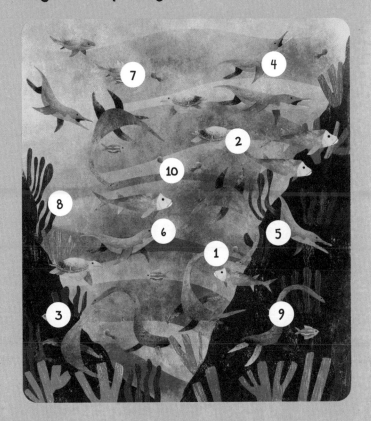

Page 45: Fierce Swimmer

Page 49: Code Crunchers

Decoded dinosaur names:

1. Massospondylus
2. Diplodocus
3. Ankylosaurus
4. Ornithomimus
5. Styracosaurus
6. Eoraptor

Page 55: Stego-Shadows

Answer: D

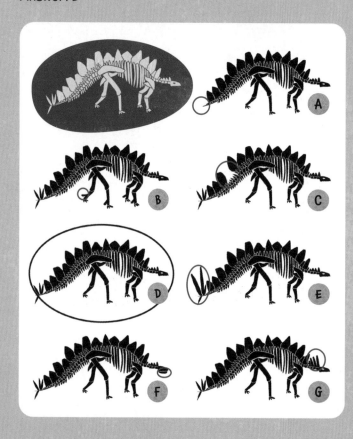

Page 57: Dino-Brain

Answers:

1-b
2-a
3 True
4-b
5-c
6 True
7-b
8-d
9 True

Page 59: Head Start

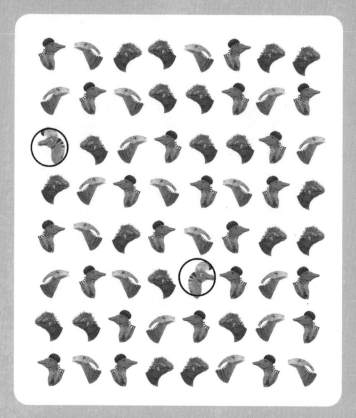

Page 63: Match Up!

Answer: 5

Page 67: Find the Ferns

Page 69: Tooth and Claw

Page 75: Taking Flight

Page 77: Who Am I?

Decoded meanings:

1. Archaeopteryx means ANCIENT WING
2. Deinonychus means TERRIBLE CLAW
3. Iguanodon means IGUANA TOOTH
4. Diplodocus means DOUBLE BEAM
5. Eoraptor means EARLY THIEF
6. Pachycephalosaurus means THICK-HEADED LIZARD

Page 79: True or False?

Answers:

1. True

2. True

3. False. The Stegosaurus died out millions of years before the Tyrannosaurus.

4. True

5. True

6. True

7. False. It is the blue whale, which is alive today.

8. False. Like all the long-necked sauropods, it was a plant-eater.

Page 81: Lost Bones

Missing T. rex bones circled below:

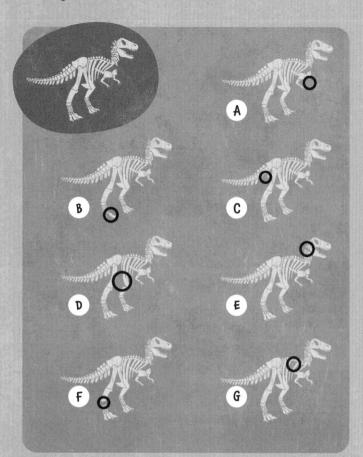

Page 85: Right Remains

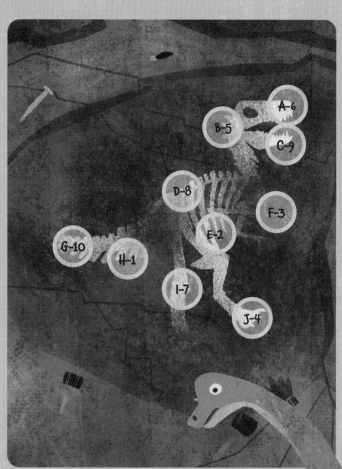